from the

GITA

Gems
from the
GITA

Commentaries on selected 160 verses containing the main teachings of GITA in simple language and lucid style

J.M. Mehta

PUSTAK MAHAL®

Publishers
Pustak Mahal®

Administrative office and sale centre
J-3/16 , Daryaganj, New Delhi-110002
☎ 23276539, 23272783, 23272784 • *Fax:* 011-23260518
E-mail: info@pustakmahal.com • *Website:* www.pustakmahal.com

Branches
Bengaluru: ☎ 080-22234025 • *Telefax:* 080-22240209
E-mail: pustak@airtelmail.in • pustak@sancharnet.in
Mumbai: ☎ 022-22010941, 022-22053387
E-mail: rapidex@bom5.vsnl.net.in
Patna: ☎ 0612-3294193 • *Telefax:* 0612-2302719
E-mail: rapidexptn@rediffmail.com

ISBN 978-81-223-1476-2

Edition: 2014

Printed at : *Ar Emm International, New Delhi*

Preface

In the whole world of literature, there is no book so elevating and inspiring as the GITA.

[Swami Sivananda]

The above opinion expressed by a renowned spiritual teacher and philosopher of recent times, declares in nutshell, the absolute supreme merit of the *GITA* which holds a unique position among the ancient scriptures of the world. Though, believed to have been written several centuries ago, yet the spiritual truths contained in this treasure house of knowledge, shall remain relevant for ever.

The *GITA* consists of eighteen chapters, comprising of seven hundred verses (Shlokas). Numerous commentaries, in several languages have already been written on the *GITA*. Most of these books are voluminous, high priced and therefore, beyond the interest and the reach of an average Indian. Consequently, the most valuable treasure of spiritual knowledge contained in these divine verses has remained hidden from the general public. Keeping this lacuna in view, an attempt has been made to produce a handy and smaller volume containing only around 160 verses which reduces the size to almost one-fifth of the original treatise. Nonetheless, all the main teachings of the Gita are covered in these selected verses. The price of the book is also kept low and within the common reach.

In short, this small book presents a simplified, handy, quick to read and understand condensed version of the *GITA*. However, all essential aspects of human life and the means to attain the highest goal of life are clearly mentioned in it. Written in easy simple language and lucid style, this book should evoke a positive response from the general English knowing readers.

J.M. Mehta,
J-186, Saket, New Delhi-110017

Contents

धर्मक्षेत्रे कुरूक्षेत्रे
Dharmakshetre Kurukshetre

It is a matter of great philosophical significance that in the first verse of the first chapter of the *Gita*, the first word is *Dharma*. The above mentioned two (or four) words can be interpreted in two ways:-

First, Kurukshetre, means the field or the land of KURUS, where the battle of *Mahabharata* was fought between the *Kauravas* and *Pandavas*, the two cousin groups. The word *Dharma Kshetre* is added to it because in this land, ancient *Rishis* performed penance and holy Yajnas. This field or land is, therefore, saturated with the spiritual atmosphere. The field of Kurukshetra is therefore considered holy and as such, is also called Dharmakshetra or the field of righteousness. Accordingly, the word Dharmakshetra has been used along with Kurukshetra.

There is also another view of these two words being associated together. Kurukshetre is a field of action. It may, therefore, be considered as symbol of human life which is also full of actions. The alignment of these two words implies that the field of action (Kurukshetra) should also be the field of Dharma (Dharmakshetre). In simple and clear terms, all actions should be performed in accordance with the principles of Dharma which means the path of righteousness, the path based on moral values. Every action in life should, therefore, be performed not with selfish motives but keeping in view the general welfare.

The central theme of the *Gita* is confined within these two words Dharamakshetre and Kurukshetra, on the basis of above interpretation. Dharma, the first word of the *Gita* is a representative of the whole philosophy enshrined in the principles of the *Gita*. One can follow Dharma, by performing one's duty by following the path of righteousness. This is the key word which indicates how human life should be lived and all its actions performed. There are ten indicators of Dharma, specified by Maharishi Manu and these can guide us on the path of righteousness.

Courage in Crisis

"YIELD NOT to this unmanliness for it does not become thee. CAST OFF this petty faint heartedness and arise"

[Verse 3 - Chapter II]

The first chapter of the *Gita* deals with the scene of battlefield at Kurukshetra, where the two opposing armies of Kauravas and Pandavas stand face to face, ready to fight. The above verse is in response to the state of utter depression and dejection of Arjuna, who was overwhelmed with grief at the prospect of killing his kith and respected teachers. Lord Krishna exhorts Arjuna not to yield to any emotional weakness in the face of crisis and instead face the challenge with courage.

The above verse provides the first practical lesson to face the challenges of real life. It is meant for the struggling humanity. The message is *Loud Clear*. DO not dishearten in the face of any difficult situation in life. The right course is to face the difficulties of life with courage, strength, manliness and proper understanding of the situation .There is no scope for mental or emotional weakness in the battle of life.

God is Supreme

"There is nothing whatsoever higher than I. All that is here is strung on Me, as rows of gems on a string."

[Verse 7 – Chapter VII]

God is one and the supreme and there is none else higher than or even equal to Him. Some ignorant people believe in many gods. This verse indicates Oneness and Unique nature of God. All constituents of creation are manifestations of God, who is the Supporter of all existence. As rows of gems are held on a string in the same way everything that exists is upheld by God, who is their Supreme Lord.

Do not Grieve

"Thou grievest for those for whom thou should not grieve for, and yet thou speakest words about wisdom. Wise men do not grieve for the dead or for the living."

[Verse 11 - Chapter II]

For vast majority, life is a general drama of grief and pain. There is a grief in case of disease, in case of failure and defeat, for loss of wealth and material possessions, in dishonour and disputes and so on. The greatest grief is felt in the case of death of a close person. If we go on multiplying these examples, it would seem that life is a large ocean of grief all around. Such grief gives rise to depression, dejection and increases the intensity of grief, all the more and thus life becomes deplorable.

The *Gita* stresses the point that there should be no place for grief either in case of death or in other situations. There is no reason to grieve over the death of the perishable body as the real Self which is the Soul, the master, does not die. Experience shows that grief makes matter worse and does not solve the difficulty. Hence, the practical way is not to grieve either for the dead or for the living.

Om (Aum) Represents God

"I am the taste in the waters. I am the light in the moon and the SUN. I am the syllable AUM in all the VEDAS; I am the sound in ether and manhood in men."

[Verse 8 – Chapter VII]

God is in everything and everywhere. He is All-pervading. The above verse gives only a few examples in which God exists, like the Sun, the Moon etc. The most significant example is of syllable OM (AUM), ओइम (ॐ) which can be written in different ways. According to the Vedas OM (AUM) is the highest name of God. Its three letter, अ, उ and म include everything God, soul and nature.

Do not Fear Death

"Just as a person casts of worn out garments and puts on others that are new, even so does the embodied soul casts off worn out bodies and takes on those that are new"

[Verse 22 - Chapter II]

"As the soul passes in the body through childhood, youth and age, even so is its taking on of another body."

[Verse 13 - Chapter II]

"To the one that is born, death is certain and certain is birth for the one that has died. Therefore, for what is unavoidable, thou should not grieve."

[Verse 13 - Chapter II]

The above verses deal with the phenomena of birth and death in a very simplified and clear cut manner.

There are several fears in human life. One fears to fall sick, to lose wealth, to meet failures and so on. On top of these fears is the Fear of Death, which is felt by most human beings except the brave.

Why fear death? The above verses of the *Gita* should be sufficient to dispel the fear of death from human mind.

In these verses, the phenomenon of death has been dealt in a very simple and natural way. In the event of death, the soul which is the real master, leaves the unfit or worn out body in order to take on a new body. So, where is the cause of fear? It is just like casting off, worn out clothes to put on new clothes.

In short, we need not fear death because of the following valid reasons:-

I. Death is a natural stage of life, like birth, childhood, youth and old age. It is a normal and natural happening.

II. Death is simply a doorway to another life. After death, the soul takes on a new body which is a change for the better.

III. Death is inevitable. There should be no reason to fear what is unavoidable.

Life Continues for Ever

"NEVER was there a time, when I was not, nor thou, nor these lords of men, nor will there ever be a time hereafter when we will all cease to be."

[Verse 12 - Chapter II]

In this verse, Lord Krishna tells Arjuna about the continuity of life process. For an average person, life is a short span between birth and death. In other words, life begins with birth and ends in death. But this is only an incorrect and short-sighted view of life and does not convey the whole reality.

The above verse unfolds the mystery of life. The *Gita* tells us that there was a life before birth and it also continues, thereafter. It persists and continues in different forms and modes and death in the present state of our existence is not the final destination. Life existed in the Past, it exists now in the Present and will continue to exist in the Future too. We should make use of the experiences gained in the past and make the best use of the present time and lay a good foundation for the future life by performing good deeds and acquiring good qualities.

The Best Devotee

"Of these, the wise ONE, who is ever in constant harmony with ME and is single-minded in devotion is the BEST – I am extremely dear to him and so is he to ME?

[Verse 17 – Chapter VII]

The fourth type of devotee mentioned in the earlier verse (16) is the Best of all devotees. Such a person is truly wise and always remains absorbed in God with absolute devotion. There is nothing else which is more dear to him than God. Such a person is also very dear to God.

Pleasure & Pain

"CONTACTS with other objects give rise to cold and heat, pleasure and pain. These come and go and do not last for ever, learn to endure these."

[Verse 14 - Chapter II]

This verse has a great significance for human life. Human life can be condensed into two words– 'Pleasure and Pain". Life is a combination of pleasant and unpleasant experiences, which are summed up as pleasure and pain. While pleasant experiences give pleasure, unpleasant ones lead to pain. Pleasure and pain are two sides of the same coin. The above verse explains the cause and nature of these and also gives instructions to deal with them. Our joys and sorrows, pleasure and pain arise out of our various activities of life, as a result of contact of our senses with the objects of the external world. Thus, our life itself provides recurring opportunities for pleasure and pain. Both are necessary accessories of our life. Where there is pleasure; there is pain too. The *Gita* tells us how to cope with these happenings of opposite nature. The way lies in the last words of this verse– learn to endure. We must go through these experiences with calm, composure and serenity of mind. ❖✪❖

Next Life

"Thinking of whatever state, he gives up his body to that being he attains, having been ever absorbed in the thought thereof."

[Verse 6 – Chapter VIII]

A person often wonders, "What will happen after death?"

Where will the soul go, after it leaves the body? The above verse gives the answer. The soul goes to that being to which the mind is set during the last moments. This will be determined by the persistent efforts of the whole life and the constant thoughts in which the mind had remained absorbed most of the time. The thoughts of the mind in the last moments, will be shaped by the thoughts and actions of the whole life. One can not control the thoughts of the mind in the last moment in a casual manner or as a result of random wishful fancy. ❖✪❖

The Wise Man

"The man, who is not troubled by these, who remains the same in pain and pleasure is wise and makes himself fit for eternal life."

[Verse 15 – Chapter II]

This verse has a close reference to the previous verse 14. We should deal with pleasant and unpleasant situations of life with an even mind. In our moments of happiness and pleasure, there is no need to jump with abnormal ostentatious expressions of excitement. Similarly in moments of pain and sorrow, one should not feel utterly miserable and unduly aggrieved and disturbed. Equanimity of mind must be maintained in both these situations. One who meets these situations of opposite nature with an even mind and remains calm and composed, is a truly wise man. In due course of time, such a man attains emancipation and trancends all pain and misery of human life.

The Immortal Soul

"He is never born, nor does he die at any time, nor having come to be will he again cease to be. He is unborn, eternal, primeval. He is not slain when the body is slain."

[Verse 20 - Chapter II]

"Weapons do not cleave this self, fire does not burn him, water does not make him wet, nor does the wind make him wet?"

[Verse 23 - Chapter II]

Human life is the combination of body and soul. While body is inert matter and is perishable, soul is conscious life element and is immortal. The above two verses briefly highlight main features of the soul which is unborn and never dies. Material weapons and strong elements of nature, like fire, water, wind etc. can not harm the soul. The verse 23 is the often quoted verse in the event of death.

The above verses express the most positive aspect of human life where soul is considered as the real master as it is ever lasting and impervious to any human. This is why really brave people like warriors. Patriots, freedom fighters and the wise are never afraid of dying for the cause for which they sacrifice their lives willingly and happily.

Dualities of Life

"TREATING ALIKE, pleasure and pain, gain and loss, victory and defeat, then get ready for battle. Thus, thou shall not incur sin."

[Verse 38 - Chapter II]

Arjuna thought that by killing his relatives and teachers he would incur sin. Lord Krishna tells him that by renouncing desire he would not incur sin.

We always have to face dualities of life. Sometime there is pleasure, sometime pain. Sometime there is gain, sometime loss, sometime success and sometime failure, and so on. In pleasure, gain and success, we feel happy, while in pain, loss and failure we are unhappy, dejected and miserable. This is not the correct way to deal with such opposing situations. The correct way to face the dualities of life lies in the first two words of the above verse, i.e. Treating Alike. This is the key formula to deal with these situations. In this way, we shall ever be prepared to fight the battle of life. While performing our duty in this manner, we shall not incur any sin and our life shall be peaceful.

Work Without Concern for the Fruits

"To ACTION ALONE, you have a right and never at all to its fruits; let not the fruits of actions be thy motives, neither let there be in you any attachment to inaction."

[Verse 47 – Chapter II]

The above verse lays down the basis of *Karma Yoga*, in a clear and concise manner. It indicates how to perform all actions in life.

One should perform one's duty or action in the best possible manner, making all efforts. While performing action, all concentration should be on the job and efforts required in its performance, without any concern for the fruits. Whatever results come forth should be accepted without any complaint or remorse. If the result is good, it shall make one happy. However, if the result is bad, one should again make greater efforts and need not just sit down, do nothing and complain. There should be no laziness or inaction in making more efforts.

Evenness of Mind is Yoga

"Fixed in Yoga, do your work, abandoning attachment, with an even mind in success and failure, for evenness of mind is YOGA."

[Verse 48 – Chapter II]

A layman often wonders 'What is Yoga?' The above verse gives a simple definition of Yoga – it is evenness of mind in all situations.

In real life, while doing any work, there is either success or failure. One should keep one's mind calm and composed in both situations. There should be no over enjoyment in success and utter dejection in failure. Thus, mind shall remain undisturbed and unperturbed and free from any attachment and its evil consequences.

Yoga is not merely physical exercises. There is a great role of interplay of mind in life. The fluctuations of mind have to be kept within proper control and that leads to yoga. This verse gives a wonderful formula for performing actions of life.

Stable Intelligence

"WHEN a man puts away all the desires of the mind, and when his spirit is content in itself, then he is called stable in intelligence."

[Verse 55 – Chapter II]

"He whose mind is untroubled in the midst of sorrows and is free from intense desire amid pleasures, he who is devoid of passion, fear and anger, is a sage of stable intelligence"

[Verse 56 – Chapter II]

The above verses highlight the conditions required to make a man stable of intelligence. Such a person has to be free from all material desires except those which are necessary for the maintenance of body and soul. Sorrows do not unduly bother such a person, who remains free from cravings in pleasure besides passion, fear and anger etc. Such a person is fully content within himself. He always remains free from selfish desires and absorbed in the contemplation of the supreme spirit.

Avoid Attachment

"When a man dwells in his mind on the sense objects, attachment is produced. Desire springs from attachment and anger evolves from desire."

[Verse 62 – Chapter II]

"ANGER leads to bewilderment and this causes loss of memory leading to destruction of intelligence, causing downfall of the individual."

[Verse 63 – Chapter II]

"ONE who keeps the senses under control, remains free from attachment and aversion, attains the purity of the spirit."

[Verse 64 – Chapter II]

Attachment is the root cause of desire which when unfulfilled leads to disappointment and anger. An angry person becomes devoid of intelligence and this leads to ruin of the individual.

In order to avoid attachment and its evil consequences, one should have full control over the senses. The soul of a person, who shuns attachment and aversion, becomes free from impurities. We should therefore avoid attachment to the objects of the senses.

Mind v/s Senses

"WHEN the mind runs after the roving sense, it carries away the understanding, in the same way as a wind carries away a boat".

[Verse 67 – Chapter II]

Senses always look outward towards external objects. When the mind goes after the sense, it is attracted by the objects of the senses and thus has no control over the faculty of understanding.

This happens like a boat which is taken away from its destination by a strong wind or a storm. The solution lies in the withdrawl of the senses from its objects. In this way, the mind shall remain under control and it will not lose its understanding.

Path to Peace of Mind

"He, who abondons all desires and acts free from longing without any sense of mineness he attains to peace."

[Verse 71 – Chapter II]

Peace of *Mind* has become a rare commodity in the modern day life, inspite of material progress and possessions. What is the way out? The above verse of the *Gita* shows the way. The formula is simple but very difficult to implement. Man is full of desires and one desire leads to another and thus he finds himself always in an intricate web of desires. As desires are insatiable, man loses his peace of mind. The way to peace lies in the abandonment of all viceous desires.

One has of course, to meet one's essential and obligatory desires. In case we can't abandon all desires, we can atleast, keep them within reasonable limit. In any case, the intense longing for anything can be curbed and we can also shun egotism. The one way to do this is to divert our attention from mundane desires and directour concentration towards the supreme. Peace of mind will surely follow.

Work Without Attachment

"WITHOUT attachment, perform always the work that has to be done. The man, who performs work without attachment, attains the highest stage.'

[Verse 19 - Chapter III]

Every one, in this world, has to do some work. Most people do work for their selfish ends to fulfil their worldly desires. Where there is desire, attachment is produced. The above verse instructs us to do work without attachment. Performing actions without attachment is of a superior level as it helps us to attain the purity of mind. Thus, work done without attachment becomes worship and it gradually leads to the highest goal of salvation.

Action is Better than Inaction

"Do thy allotted work, for action is better than inaction. Even the maintenance of the physical existence is not practicable without action."

[Verse 8 – Chapter III]

The above verse highlights the importance of action which is better than lack of action. It is a fact of human nature that one is always engaged in some action. It is always better to do something useful then just sit idle.

There is a saying that an idle mind is devils' worship. One must, therefore, always remain engaged in doing one's duty which comes to him either by choice or otherwise. An important example from our life is that we have to take suitable action even for our physical existence. It will not be possible to maintain human life, by doing nothing. Action is, therefore, always better than inaction which is sheer laziness.

Two–fold Way of Life

"In this world, a two-fold way of life has been taught by Me, the path of knowledge for men of contemplation and that of works for men of action".

[Verse 3 - Chapter III]

There are two main types of seekers in this world, introverts who look within through contemplation and extroverts whose natural tendency is to work in the external world. The first type think deeply, meditate, analyze and thus follow the path of knowledge. The second type are actively engaged in the outside activities and thus follow the path of action. But this distinction is not exclusive as men of action need knowledge and those, who follow the path of knowledge are also engaged in some sort of action. What matters is the predominance of one tendency over the other which makes a specific type. Both these paths if followed effectively and resolutely can lead to liberation.

Follow the Great men

"Whatever a greatman does, the same is done by others, as well. The world follows the standard set by him."

[Verse 21 – Chapter III]

It is often noticed that whatever is done by leaders or greatmen in a society, the same is followed by common people. That is how great movements or religions started by greatmen become mass movements such as freedom movements, sects and religions etc., as these, gather millions of folowers. As greatmen become path makers, it is utmost necessary that the greatmen and public leaders must set right and desirable standards so that common people are not led astray and they are on the right track of righteousness.

Control Desires

"Enveloped is wisdom by the insatiable fire of desire which is the constant foe of the wise."

[Verse 39 – Chapter III]

"The senses, the mind and the intelligence are said to be its seat, covering wisdom by these, it deludes the soul."

[Verse 40 – Chapter III]

"Therefore, control thy senses from the beginning and slay this sinful destroyer of wisdom and discrimination."

[Verse 41 – Chapter III]

Desire is never satisfied by the enjoyment of its objects. If one desire is satisfied temporarily it leads to more and more and to another desire. It increases like the fire to which fuel is added. Thus, desire acts as a constant enemy of the wise. Desire gets support from the senses, the mind and intelligence, all of which, under its influence, delude the soul which gets misguided.

The last verse (41) shows the way to get ride of the binding effect of desire. One must control the Senses from the very start, as soon as the desire is about to arise. The saying "Nip the evil in the bud" has to be implemented. Desire must, therefore, be curbed at the initial stage for the safety of wisdom and intelligence.

Levels of Consciousness

"The SENSES are great, the MIND is greater than the senses, greater than the mind is intelligence (Buddhi), but the SPIRIT is above the intelligence."

[Verse 42 – Chapter III]

The above verse indicates a hierarchy of levels of strength of conscious control. The roving senses are quite powerful but a careful mind can exercise its control over the senses. However, when the mind and the senses hold their sway, it is the intelligence which can control the mind and the senses both. We attain the highest power of consciousness or freedom when the intelligence is guided by the light of the supreme Spirit. In this manner, guided by the Higher Self, we can control our desires which arise from the lower self. This is how we can attain the highest level of freedom through the gradual and progressive control of our various levels of consciousness.

God Realisation

"Those, whose mind and intellect are wholly absorbed in God, who constantly remain identified with HIM and for whom. HE is the sole object of devotion, they reach the eternal state of God-realisation and their sins are wiped out with wisdom."

[Verse 17 – Chapter III]

God can be realised through unfailing constant devotion. In such a state, mind and intellect always look and think for God. The devotee thinks of God everywhere, All-pervading. God becomes the main object of life and in due course, the devotee reaches the highest stage of God-realisation. As a result of affinity with the Almighty Lord, all his sins are destroyed with the acquisition of divine wisdom, bestowed by God. True devotion is the fastest means of God realisation.

The Way to Salvation

"FREE from passion, fear and anger, absorbed in Me taking refuge in Me, many purified by the practice of wisdom, have attained Me."

[Verse 10 – Chapter IV]

The above verse shows the way to salvation which is the highest goal of human life. Most people wish to attain God but do not qualify themselves by making right efforts. In order to attain God, one has to, first of all, purify himself by the practice of right knowledge through right understanding. One has also to purge himself of the evils of passion, fear and anger and then meditate on God with full devotion and dedication. The way to salvation or God-realisation lies through complete surrender to the Almighty Lord.

The Four-fold Order of Society

"The four-fold order was created by Me, according to the division of quality and work."

[Verse 13 – Chapter IV]

The origin of the creation of four types of individuals by God is found in the *Veda*. The *Gita* supports this view. The basis of this division of mankind is neither birth nor heredity. The emphasis is on *guna* (quality or aptitude) and *karma* (work) performed by an individual. The order or the *varna* to which a person really belongs is independent of sex, birth in a particular family, it is determined by temperament and vocation one follows. It is assumed that the whole mankind was originally of one class but later on it became divided into four classes or types on account of quality, nature and work performed by different individuals. The present division of society into four castes on the basis of heredity is artificial, man made and is based on the vested interests of ignorant and selfish well-entrenched groups of society.

Abandon Attachment

"He who works abondoning attachment, offering his actions to God, is not tainted by sin, like a LOTUS remains untouched by water."

[Verse 10 – Chapter V]

The peculiarity of Lotus is that though it is found in the water, it rises above and remains untouched by it. In the same way, a person who performs his actions without attachment to their fruits, remains untouched by sin. Such a person does not shun works but performs them as an offering to the Almighty Lord. He does not act for any selfish reasons and therefore renounces attachment. Consequently, he is not touched by sin.

Decline of Righteousness

"Whenever there is decline of righteousness and rise of unrighteousness, I send forth myself."

[Verse 8 – Chapter IV]

"The SUPREME though unborn and unborn and undying incarnates himself in human form, from time to time, to uphold righteousness and to destroy wickedness."

[Verse 9 – Chapter IV]

The above two verses support the phenomenon of incarnation of God in human form in certain desired circumstances. When righteousness vanishes and unrighteousness rises, the supreme spirit is born in human form to destroy wickedness and to spread the supremacy of righteousness. The coming of God in human form is known as '*Avatara*' which implies that the divine comes down to the worldly level to overthrow the forces of evil and unrighteousness. In Hindu religion, Lord Rama and Lord Krishna are believed to be such '*Avataras*'. They were manifestation of God in human form, who appeared in the world to destroy wickedness (Adharma).

Established in God

"He, who neither rejoices on obtaining what is pleasant, nor grieves on getting what is unpleasant, and who is stable in understanding and unbewildered is established in God."

[Verse 20 – Chapter V]

The above verse shows the way how to become established in God. An average person becomes overjoyed on getting something pleasant and gets sorrowful on abtaining what is unpleasant. Such a person remains deluded with the material world and is therefore away from God. But a person who remains the same in both pleasant and unpleasant situations because of his firm intellect or stable understanding, establishes affinity with God. One should, therefore, practise an attitude of even mindedness in dealing with opposite situations in real life. This is the way to eternal bliss.

Real Happiness

"When the SOUL is no longer attached to external objects, one obtains the real happiness in the inner-self. Such a person becomes self-disciplined in Yoga and attains eternal bliss."

[Verse 21 – Chapter V]

Man craves for real happiness but does not get it becauses he gropes in the dark and explores it in his contacts with the external objects of the world. He may procure money, material possessions, name and fame in his worldly pursuits but not the real happiness. For achieving real happiness, one has to get detached from the bondage of the senses. Having done so through the discipline of yoga, one can get concentrated on God and attain real happiness. Freedom from the senses and their objects paves the way to eternal bliss, which lies in the inner-self and not in the external world and its fantasies.

Worldly Pleasures

"Whatever pleasures are born of worldly contacts are sources of sorrow, they have a beginning and an end, no wise man delights in them."

[Verse 22 – Chapter V]

All pleasures of the wold lead to sorrow. These pleasures which are born of contacts with the external objects are of temporary in nature. They begin at a point, continue for sometime and then have their end. These temporary pleasures , in their absence are preceded by sorrow or pain and as they end are followed by sorrow and pain. Those who are wise and have proper understanding are not tempted by these mundane pleasures and they do not delight in them. One should , therefore, not be misguided by such pleasures which seem pleasant to start with but end in sorrow.

True Happiness Lies Within

He, who finds happiness within and is content in itself, he becomes devine and attains the beatitude of GOD."

[verse 24 - Chapter V]

THE holy men whose sins are destroyed, whose doubts and dualities are cut and minds are disciplined and who rejoice in the welfare of all creatures attain to the beatitude of GOD.

[verse 25 - Chapter V]

The above two verses clearly indicate the way to eternal bliss. One must first understand that the true happiness lies within and not in the pursuits of external world. The pleasures obtained from contacts with the external world are only temporary and sources of sorrow, Those who are free from evils and whose minds have attained purity of yogic discipline and who work for the welfare of all creatures attain to eternal bliss.

How to Meditate?

DETACHED from all external objects, fixing the gaze between the eyebrows, making even the inward and outward breaths moving within the nostrils, the devotee who has controlled the senṣes, mind and understanding, who is intent on liberation, who has cast away desire, fear and anger is ever freed.'

[Verses 27, 28 - Chapter V]

The above verse shows how to meditate by concentrating the vision between the eyebrows and upon the indward and outgoing breath. In this manner, by long practice and self-control one can seek liberation. These are certain pre-conditions required to be met, as follows:-

1 Detachment from the external world.
2. Strong determination to attain liberation.
3. Full control over mind, senses and proper understanding.
4. Frcedone from desire, fear and anger.

Self-mastery

ONE who has conquered ones mind and has attained the calm of self-mastery in the midst of dualities, such as cold and heat, pleasure and pain etc., he remains in constant communion with the SUPREME-SELF.'

[Verse 7 - Chapter. V1]

Self Mastery is the means to God-realisation. This goal is attained when one conquers the raving tendencies of the mind and has complete control over the senses. Our life is a combination of experiences of opposite effects, such as pleasure and pain, comforts and discomforts etc. when a man attains complete control over these dualities of life, he remains the same in these opposite situations which do not disturb his calm. This is the stage of self-mastery which leads to the constant communion with the Supreme Spirit, This is the state of blessedness where the consequences of opposites of life do not adversely affect him.

Self is the Lord of the Self

"LET a man lift himself, let him not degrade himself, for the self alone is the friend of the self and the self alone is the enemy of the self."

[Verse.5 - Chapter .V1]

"For him, who has conquered his self by the SELF his self is a friend, but for him who has not possessed his SELF, his own self acts his foe ."

[Verse. 6 - Chapter . V1]

A man lives at the level of two stage of consciousness – the lower and the higher. At the lower level, he identifies himself with the material world through the body, mind, the senses and the intellect etc. At the lower level of consciousness he degrades himself by doing wrong acts, committing sins etc. When he raises himself above the lower level, he identifies with the higher level of devine consciousness In the latter case, he conquers his lower self by the Higher self and his own self gets subdued and becomes his friend. Without the affinity of the Higher Self, the lower self misguides and becomes the enemy. These verses teach us the way to self-development which lies through self-effort. It is your own efforts which lead to progress and self-improvement. If we exercise self-control, our lower self becomes a friend, otherwise to goes astray and becomes an enemy. The importance of self-mastery has been emphasised in these verses.

The Way to Reach God (II)

"Fix thy mind on Me; be devoted to Me; sacrifice to Me; so thou shall come to Me. I promise thou truly, for thou art dear to ME."

[Verse 65 – Chapter XVIII]

Lord Krishna tells Arjuna, the way to reach Him. It is through concentration of mind on God, complete devotion and surrender to Him, that one can reach the Supreme. Thoughts, worship, sacrifice and reverence, all these acts and feelings should be directed to Him. In this way, the devotee will attract the grace and love of God and will surely reach Him.

Mental Discipline

"Let the YOGI constantly concentrate his mind, remaining in solitude, self-controlled, free from desires and cravings for material possessions."

[VERSE 10 - Chapter. VI.]

This verse briefly describes the discipline of meditation on God. Here, the constant concentration of mind on God is required. For this, it is necessary to remain alone, self-controlled and unagitated. Desire and longings for material possessions are causes of disturbance of the mind. One should, therefore, remain free from these. It is necessary to divert one's mind from the material world and direct it towards God. These should be no craving for material possessions and mundane pleasures. Living alone, in solitude, as far as practicable is very helpful for mental discipline. One should keep God in mind always, while performing various activities of life. It will make concentration on God easier, while sitting in the actual process of meditation.

Self-discipline

"The man who is temperate in food and recreation, who practices restraint in his actions, acquires self-discipline which removes sorrow."

[Verse 17 – Chapter VI]

This verse gives a few tips for self-discipline which leads to avoid sorrow. Practice of moderation in all requirements for existence, such as, food, drinks, entertainment, sleep etc. is the key to self-discipline. What is required is the practice of Restraint in these things and other actions of life. One should remain within beneficial proper limit and avoid all sorts of temptations to have more and more. Complete abstinence is not called for moderation and self-restraint, are the key factiors for self-discipline.

Perfect Yoga

"When the disciplined mind is established in the SELF, free from all desires, then one gets harmonised in yoga."

[Verse 18 – Chapter VI]

"That state when thought is at rest,controlled by the practice of concentration, when one beholds the SELF through the self and experiences bliss."

[Verse 20 – Chapter VI]

"The state of disconnection from pain is Yoga which should be practised with full determination and dedication."

[Verse 23 – Chapter VI]

The above verses briefly describe the state of perfect yoga and how it can be attained. Abandonment of all selfish desires, practice of concentration, control of mind, full determination are the main means to attain this state, in which there is no movement of thought and the inner self-experiences the bliss of the Supreme Self. This is the state of blessedness where there is complete freedom from pain. The discipline of Yoga has to be practised with determination and without any slackness.

Supreme Happiness

"SUPREME happiness comes to the yogi whose mind is peaceful, whose passions are at rest, who is free from sin and has become one with GOD."

[Verse 27 – Chapter VI]

The above verse mentions following conditions for the highest state of happiness which comes with the experience of God:-

1. Peaceful mind.
2. Absence of craving
3. Freedom from sins.

Such a state can be achieved through constant long practice, after attaining perfection with the gradual progress of many lives.

Restless Mind

"Without doubt, the mind is restless and difficult to restrain, but it can be controlled by constant practice and non-attachment."

[Verse 35 – Chapter VI]

The mind which is always rooing is, no doubt, restless. The tendencies of mind are always fluctuating. But inspite of its impulsive nature, control over mind is possible though extremely difficult. Two fundamental conditions to control the mind are constant long practice and an attitude of non-attachment. The senses which are the instruments of the mind to establish contacts with the external objects have to be kept under complete control of the mind. The mind has to become the master of the senses and not their share in order to cultivate the attitude of non-attachment. When this is done, constant practice will do the rest to establish control over the restless mind.

Two Natures of God

"EARTH, water, fire, air and ether, mind understanding and self-souse - this is the eight-fold division of my nature.

[Verse 4 – Chapter VII]

"This is my lower nature, My higher nature is the SOUL by which this world is upheld."

[Verse 5 – Chapter VII]

"Everything originates from these natures. I am the origin of this world and its disscolution also.

[Verse 6 – Chapter VII]

These verses show how the whole creation is constituted. God is the creator of this world and its destroyer as well. He has two natures or aspects, lower and Higher. Between these two natures, all existence is included, conscious and unconscious. The lower nature is eight-fold and consists of all that is unconscious. The High nature is the Soul or consciousness which operates at two level – the super soul and the individual soul. The whole world is the field of operation of the Soul. Everything originates from these two natures and God is their origin and operator.

Devotees of God

"The devotees of God are of four types, the man in distress, the seeker of knowledge, the seeker for wealth, and the man of WISDOM."

[Verse 16 – Chapter VII]

Those who worship God are of four types, as follows:-

1. Those who face some difficulty and suffer from some pain due to some diseases or unpleasant circumstances etc.
2. Those who are devout and wish to know the Truth, the reality of existence etc.
3. Those who are desirous of wealth, material possessions, material success, honour etc.
4. Those who seek nothing and are full of devotion for God. They are single-minded and worship God for his own sake and not for any selfish reasons. The are men of true Wisdom.

The first three categories are desirous of something, some rewards or favours but the fourth category seeks nothing and refuses nothing. He seeks only the Supreme in a spirit of self-surrender.

Creation and Dissolution

"All beings, pass into nature which is My own, at the end of the cycle; and at the beginning of the next cycle, I send them forth."

[Verse 7 – Chapter IX]

The cycle of creation and dissolution of the universe happens as the day follows the night. At the end of each creation, all beings are dissolved in the nature of the Creator and at the appropriate time again, at the beginning of the next creation, God again sends them forth. This process is eternal and has no beginning or an end.

Remember God Always

"Whosoever, at the time of death, gives up his body to depart, thinking of ME alone, he attains Me, there is no doubt about it."

[Verse 5 – Chapter VIII]

A person who remembers God at the time of death attains HIM. But this is not as easy as it seems. It is not always possible to think of God at the time of death. Most people think of their wealth and property, their children and relatives, their past happenings etc. during their lost moments. It is only a rare person, who sincerely remembers God at the time of his departure from the world. Only that person will think of God in such situation, who has been constantly remembering God with full devotion in his previous days. The importance of the state of mind is emphasised in this verse. In order to achieve the desirable end of God realisation, one has to remember God always throughout life. Only then, one will be in a position to think of Him at the time of death.

The Way to Supreme

"He who meditates on the SUPREME with his thought attained by constant practice and not wandering for anything else, he reaches the supreme."

[Verse 8 – Chapter VIII]

The way to God-realisation lies in single-minded devotion which comes from constant practice. This state is achived when one gets absorbed in the thought of the Supreme. Most human beings generally remain involved in the routined activities of life and in the fulfillment of worldly desires. In the circumstances, there is hardly any time for meditation on God. We often hear the general complaint when people say that they have no time for meditation and all their time is spent in solving their problems of everyday life. First, one should inculcate a keen inclination towards the spiritual path then concentrate one's thought on the Supreme with full devotion and dedication. Only then, with constant practice, over a longtime, one can hope to experience the Supreme Reality.

Om – The Doorway to God

"He who utters the single syllable AUM (which is GOD) remembering ME, as he departs, leaving his body, goes to the highest goal."

[Verse 13 – Chapter VIII]

OM (AUM) (ॐ) is the highest name of GOD. Remembering OM means remembering God. One who remembers OM at the time of his death will attain God. This seems to be an easy way to attain the highest goal but it is really not so. Most people forget God and think of many worldly things at the time of death. Only those who are attened to God, through the constants practice of yogic discipline in the whole life. Will utter the name of God during their last moments. For them, remembering OM (AUM) at the time of death will act as doorway to God realisation.

Constant Meditation

"He who constantly meditates on ME, thinking of none else, who is ever disciplned in yoga, by him I am easily reached."

[Verse 14 – Chapter VIII]

This verse echoes a similar idea as contained in the earlier verse 13. Constant meditation on God is an easy way to reach God. But it is not easy to practise constant meditation. Only those devotees will become adept in meditation, who have mastered the extremely difficult discipline of Yoga which has to be adopted life long. Constant meditation implies complete absorption in the thought of God without going astray. God is the only adorable object of meditation and one who practices constant meditation resulting from life-long practice of yogic discipline surely attains GOD.

The Incarnate Supreme Reality

"By ME, all this universe is pervaded through My unmanifest form. All beings abide in ME but I do not abide in them."

[Verse 4 – Chapter IX]

The beauty of this verse lies in the fact that it clearly and very briefly depicts some of the main attributes of God. He is All-pervading and invisible. God is invisible but pervades in all creations. He is also the Supporter of all existence which abides in Him. Strangely though, the forms of the universe do not adequately express Him. His incarnate, supreme reality is above the appearance of shapes and forms of material objects although we may draw some inference from them of His pervasiveness. God is everywhere and all objects subsist in Him but He is above all of them. ❖✪❖

Merits of Meditation

"Those who worship ME, meditating on ME ALONE, who persevere constantly. I grant them their needs and security in what they have."

[Verse 22 – Chapter IX]

True worship of God has its own rewards. God looks after the genuine requirements and the safety of His devoties. If we surrender overselves completely to God and worship Him Alone, with full devotion, He will not let us down. In this way, we can depend upon the mercy of God and his saving care and inspiring grace. But constant perseverance in true worship and single-minded devotion to the Almighty. Lord is pre-requisite to deserve attainment of due merits and rewards. It is necessary to abandon all other attachments and love to attain love and care of God. ❖✪❖

Devotion Matters

"Whosoever offers to ME, with devotion, a leaf, a flower, a fruit or water, that offering of love of the pure of heart, I accept."

[Verse 26 – Chapter IX]

God accepts all offerings made with devotion by pure-hearted persons. Here the emphasis is on two things– love and devotion with which the offering is made and the purity of heart of the devotee. The true value of the offering made lies in the intensity of love and devotion with which the offering is made and not on the value and quality of the object which is offered. However, low in value the offering, if it is made by a pure hearted person even though he is poor or low in worldly station, with great love and earnestness, it is acceptable to God. What really matters is devotion and the purity of heart of the devotee.

Effect of Self-surrender

"With the mind firmly set on the way of renunciation, you will be free from the bondage of actions having good and bad results. Thus, having completely surrendered yourself (all actions), you shall attain Me."

[Verse 28 – Chapter IX]

The way to attain God lies in the complete surrender of all actions to God, with a spirit of renunciation. All worldly actions, good or bad have their favourable or unfavourable effects. These lead to bondage. But actions performed with the attitude of disinterestedness for their fruits and with the spirit of complete surrender to God do not lead to bondage. Such actions are self-less, performed as an offering to God and without any concern for their fruits, lead to emancipation.

God is for All

"Those who take refuge in ME, though they may be lowly born, women. Vaisyas and Sudras, they also attain the highest goal."

[Verse 32 – Chapter IX]

God is open to all, without distinction of sex or caste, birth etc. This verse repudiates the impression created by some orthodox selfish priests that men of higher castes only can attain the highest goal. The message of the *GITA* gets beyond man-made distinctions of race, gender, caste etc. It lays emphasis on spiritual values. The gates of God-realisation are open to all who take refuge in Him, with love, devotion and spirit of complete self-surrender.

Worship God Alone

On Me fix thy mind, to ME he devoted, worship ME, thus making yourself steadfast in ME and completely surrendering to ME, you shall attain ME."

[Verse 34 – Chapter IX]

This verse very briefly, sums up how to attain God. One has to completely concentrate his mind on God alone. There is no scope for wondering around here and there and running after other gods and material goals. God alone has to be the single-minded object of steadfast, worship and devotion. All actions have to be dedicated to Him, in a spirit of self-surrender, having no worldly desires and attachments. A true devotee always remains absorbed in God and is satisfied with what God does to him, without any complaints and regrets. In this way, one can surely attain God.

God is the Creator

"I am the origin of all; from ME, the whole creation proceeds, knowing this, the wise worship ME with devotion and reverence."

[Verse 8 – Chapter X]

The above verse in nutshell gives the knowledge of GOD the All-pervading. He is the source of all creation. He is the creator and the operator of the whole universe. The entire universe which includes numerous forms and shapes is His manifestation. A wise person who knows the reality of God is not deluded by different forms and shapes but he remains attuned to the origin, the CREATOR. One who has the real knowledge of God, in this manner, worships Him alone with full conviction, understanding and devotion.

Grace of God

"Those who worship ME with consistent devotion and love, I grant them concentration of understanding by which they reach ME."

[Verse 10 – Chapter X]

In order to reach God, it is essential to worship Him with utter unselfish love and steadfast devotion. In such a state, a true devotee remains absorbed in the thought of God. His mind is set on Him without any wavering and he gains tranquility in all situations, pleasant or unpleasant. To such devotees, God grants spiritual wisdom by which he sees God in everything. This is the state of God-realisation which comes through the grace of God.

Om (Aum) Represents God

"Of the great sages, I am BHRIGU, of speech. I am the single syllable AUM (ॐ); of offerings I am the offering of silent meditation, and of unmovable things. I am the Himalaya."

[Verse 25 – Chapter X]

Three points are very significant in this verse, as follows:-

1. AUM (OM) (ॐ) is the symbol of GOD. It is the highest name of God.
2. Silent meditation, which implies the constant repetition of God's name, with full understanding and devotion is the best form of offering to God.
3. It shows the importance of Himalaya. It is not merely the mountain, it shows the might the grandeur, and the sublime nature of the Lord.

Of course, saint Bhrigu, being a great devotee of God possessing His glory and wisdom is dear to God.

Devotion is the Best Means

"By unsweving devotion to ME, I can be known truly seen and entered into."

[Verse 54 – Chapter XI)

The importance of devotion has been repeatedly emphasised in many earlier verses of the *Gita*. This verse sums up the value of devotion in a concise manner. In nut shell, unswerving devotion is the Key to God-realisation. But the devotion has to be single-minded, unswerving and steadfast. The ideal devotee becomes restless to realise only One object, God. He constantly thanks of God, adores Him, looks upon Him with all his mind, senses and the spirit. In this way, he experiences God, truly understands Him and finally attains Him.

The Essence of Devotion

"He who performs actions for ME, who makes ME his goal, who worships ME free from attachment, who is without malice towards all beings, attains ME."

[Verse 55 – Chapter XI]

This verse shows the essence of devotion. One must earnestly perform one's duty, surrendering all actions to God and free from all worldly attachments. He should also be free from enmity or bad feelings for other creatures. One should become an instrument of God while performing his actions. God becomes the only goal and the devotee entirely depends upon Him. And finally, reaches the stage, when he says "I am God's and God is mine." This is the highest stage and essence of devotion to God.

Different Ways to Reach God

In CHAPTER XII. the GITA tells us to approach God in different ways, as briefly mentioned in the following verses:-

I. Fix thy mind and understanding on ME...

[Verse – 8]

II. Seek to reach me by the practice of concentration.

[Verse 9]

III. Perform all actions for My sake with the aim to serve Me...

[Verse 10]

IV. Renounce the fruit of action and take refuge in ME...

[Verse II]

Man can try to reach God in different ways as briefly indicated in the above verses.

First, he can set his mind and understanding on God in a stead fast manner. If this is found difficult, then one can try the method of concentration through long practice. If this is not practicable then the way of service may help, performing all actions for the sake of God. If this is also not found feasible then one should take refuge in God, with a spirit of complete self-surrender and renunciation, in all humility. One can try these methods and practice one which is found most suitable.

Different Methods – A Comparison

"BETTER indeed is knowledge than practice; better than knowledge is meditation, better than meditation is the renunciation of the fruit of action; on renunciation follows immediately, peace."

[Verse 12 – Chapter XII]

These are four independent methods for God realisation. This verse briefly shows their comparison. Thus, meditation is better than knowledge which is better than the practice of concentration. Of all these, the renunciation of the fruit of action is must useful as it leads to divine peace immediately. It is observed that knowledges meditation and concentration are more difficult than the renunciation of the fruit of action. The last brings about inner calm and peace which is fundamental to God realisation. ❖✪❖

Three Paths

"Some perceive the SELF in the self by the self through meditation, others through the path of knowledge and still others by the path of action"

[Verse 24 – Chapter XIII]

This verse indicates three paths to God-realisation. These are through meditaion, knowledge and action. These are also known as Bhakti Yoga, Gyan Yoga and Karma Yoga. Which path an individual follows depends upon his intrinsic nature or personal temperament. An action-oriented person should follow the path of action – which means selfless action. A man of contemplative nature will follow the path of knowledge. Similarly, a man of faith and devotion will follow the path of meditation. However, these paths are not water-tight compartments and are not to be practiced in isolation as these are inter-linked. ❖✪❖

Whom God Loves Most

"Those devotees, who follow with FAITH, holding ME as their SUPREME aim, this eternal wisdom, are exceedingly dear to ME.

[Verse 20 – Chapter XII]

This is the last verse of Chapter XII of the *Gita*. It makes distinction between devotees, who are dear to God (as mentioned in verse 13 to 19) and those who are exceedingly dear to Him.

Faith plays a very important role in the path of devotion. When a devotee regards the Lord as his supreme goal, he is naturally inspired to practise the path of spiritual disciplne, by Gods' grace. The more a devotee is inclined towards God, the more the virtues are revealed in him and the vices vanish. Such a devotee depends upon God completely, as an innocent baby on mother. God is his beloved and therefore he is exceedingly dear to Him.

True Knowledge

"KNOW ME as the knower of the FIELD in all fields. The knowledge of the field and its knower, is true knowledge.

[Verse 2 - Chapter XIII)

The body is called the FIELD and one who knows it, is called knower of the field. The body passes through birth, growth and death and all events take place in it. However, the All-pervading principle in the body, remaining unattached just witnesses all these happenings. He sees and knows all that is happening in the field. He is, therefore, the Knower of the field. At the universal level, God is the known of all the fields. Thus, the knowledge of the field and its knower is considered as tree knowledge.

The Field (Kshetra)

"The FIVE gross elements (earth, fire, water, air and ether) Ego, ten sense organs and mind, five organs of knowing (eyes, ears, nose, tongue and skin)- five organs of action and the five objects of the senses (sight, smell, hearing, taste and touch), the unmanifest (NATURE) and intellect (MAHAT)."

"Desire and hatred, pleasure and pain, the aggregate (the organism), intelligence and steadfastness described, this in brief is the FIELD along with its modifications."

[Verse 5,6 - Chapter XIII)

The above 24 principles, besides some other mental states mentioned in verse 6 are the constituents of the Field. The field is subject to change. It is born, it grows, stays, produces, decays and at last dies. The field is of non-permanent nature.

Nature and Spirit (Soul)

"Know thou that nature (prakriti) and soul are both without beginning and the forms and modes are born of nature. Nature is said to be the cause of all activities of the body and its organs while soul is the cause of experience of pleasure and pain."

[Verses 19-20 – Chapter XIII]

According to *Gita*, Prakriti is the lower nature and the Spirit (Soul) is the higher nature of the Supreme Lord. God is eternal and so are prakriti and soul. The body and the senses are produced by prakriti and the soul is said to be the cause of experiencing pleasure and pain. The soul, by nature is blissful but when it identifies itself with the objects of nature, it is stained by joy and sorrow, pleasure and pain.

Knowledge is Practice of Virtures

Verses 7 to 11 of Chapter XIII of the *Gita* mention Twenty (20) moral virtues which constitute knowledge. Which includes the Practice of these virtues and not its more theoretical learning. By the development of these moral virtues, a devotee discriminates between the ever changeless SELF and the passing forms of the body (field). Without following the spiritual discipline (practice of these virtues), a devotee can not realize the reality and thus ignorance prevails. These 20 moral virtues are as follows:-

Humility (Absence of pride), integrity (absence of deceit) non-violence, forgivness, uprightness, service to the teacher, purity of body and mind, steadfastness and self control.

[Verse 7]

Indifference to the object of the senses, absence of egoism (self-effacement), perception of the evil and misery of birth, death and old age, and disease.

[Verse 8]

Non-attachment, non-identification of the self with son, wife, home and the like and even-mindedness to all desirable and undesirable happenings.

[Verse – 9]

Unswerving devotion to God. With whole-hearted dependence on Him, inclination for solitary places and dislikes for the crowd of people.

[Verse 10]

Constancy in the knowledge of the SUPREME SPIRIT, seeing God everywhere as the object of true knowledge – this is declared to be knowledge, and what is contrary to its is non-knowledge (ignorance).

[Verse – 11]

The practice of above 20 virtues enahles us to realize the TRUTH, the ultimate Reality and to know the difference between the field (Ksktra) and the knower of the field (Kslatrajna). This is knowledge and the opposite to it is ignorance.

The Knower of the Field

Verses 12 to 17 of Chapter XIII of the *Gita* briefly describe the Knower of the field. He is the Supreme Lord by knowing whom, life eternal is attained. Main points are as follows:-

He is without beginning and end.

He is All-pervading, encompassing all.

He is devoid of senses, yet appears to have the qualities of all the senses.

He is detached, yet supports all.

He is outside as well as inside all beings. He is moving as also unmoving. He is too subtle to be grasped.

He is far, yet very near.

He is indivisible, yet seems to devided among all beings.

He is the creator, sustainer and destroyer of beings.

He is the Light of all lights, beyond all darkness. He is knowledge, the object of knowledge and is known by knowledge itself. He dwells in every one's heart.

Thus, in Chapter XIII, the nature of the field, the knowledge and the knower of the field are briefly described. The devotee, who comprehends this, becomes fit to reach God.

Cause of Birth

> **"The SOUL being amidst nature, enjoys the modes of nature, gets attached to them and due to this association, takes birth in good on bad wombs accordingly'.**
>
> *[Verse 21 – Chapter XIII]*

The Soul seated in the midst of nature, forgets its real-self and identifies itself with the modes of nature and enjoys pleasure and pain. In this way, it gets attached to the modes of nature and this attachment becomes the cause of future births in good and evil bodies. Good wombs are those where there is much pleasure while bad ones are those where there is much pain.

The Supreme Spirit is the Witness

"The SUPREME SPIRIT in the body is the WITNESS, the PERMITTER, the supporter, the experience, the Great LORD and the SUPREME SELF."

[Verse 22 – Chapter XIII]

Besides the nature and the individual soul, the Supreme Spirit in the body observes the modes of nature and acts as a witness. He is the all-pervading, the controller, the supporter, the Experience. So He is called the Great Lord and the Supreme Self. Which is different from the individual self; the latter gets entangled in the activities of prakriti.

Dear to God

"He who has no ill will to any being, who is friendly and compassionate, free from ego and self-pride, even murded in pain and pleasure...

[Verse 13]

"He, who is ever content, self-controlled, steadfast, with mind and understanding firmly ser on ME...

[Verse 14]

These verses mention the qualities of a devotee, who is dear to God. These are other verses (15 to 20) which mention other qualities, as well.

These are summarised below:-

Who is free from fear and agitation.

Who has no expectation, pure, unconcerned and untroubled, skilful in action. One who renounces the fruit of all action.

Who neither rejoices nor hates, neither grieves nor causes grief.

Who is same to friend and foe, and is same in dualities and is free from attachments.

Who is content with anything that comes his way, restrained in speech and firm in mind.

In general, these are the main qualities which enable a devotee to come close to God.

Three Gunas (Modes, Sattava, Rajas, Tamas)

"The Three modes (GUNAS), goodness (sattava), passion (RAJAS) and dullness (TAMAS), born of nature (PRAKRITI), find down in the body, the imperishable dweller (SOUL) in the body."

[Verse 5 – Chapter XIV]

The modes (Gunas) are the three tendencies of nature (prakriti) which form the basis of all substances. There influence the soul and lead it to the cycle of birth and death, when the latter indentifies itself with the former. In this way, the soul gets into bondage. In order to get out of bondage, the soul has to rise above the hold of gunas.

Effect of Modes (Gunas)

"OF there, goodness (sattava) being pure, causes Illumination and is flowless. It besides by attachment to happiness and knowledge."

[Verse 6 – Chapter XIV]

"PASSION (Rajas) is the source of longing and attachment. It binds the soul by attachment to action."

[Verse 7 - Chapter XIV)

"Dullness (Tamas) is born of ignorance and deludes all embodied beings. It binds the soul through negligence, indolence and sleep."

[Verse 8 – Chapter XIV)

There verses show the effects of gunas upon the soul. Sattava though causes desire for noble objects, produces attachment for happiness and knowledge. Due to predominance of sattava an individual gets attached to pleasure and peace and thus becomes bound.

Rajas produces cravings for attachment to persons, things and actions. It evolves from thirst and attachment and binds the soul through attachment for activities and their fruits. Tamas is far inferior to other gunas. It is born of ignornace and foolishness and deludes the soul which loses discrimination between right and wrong.

Goodness (Sattava) attaches one to happiness, passion (Rajas) to action and Tamas to delusion. Thus, all these gunas have binding effects.

Predominance of Gunas

"Goodness (Sattava) brings happiness, passion (Rajas) leads to action but dullness (Tamas) veils wisdom and attaches to negligence."

[Verse 9 – Chapter XIV)

The three gunas are present in all human beings though in different proportion. In each embodied soul, one on the other guna predominates and thus produces different results. The dominating guna has its consequences accordingly, as mentioned in the above verse.

Goodness prevails when the hight of knowledge streams forth.

When Rajas increases, greed, activity, unrest and craving spring up.

When dullness predominates, inactivity, negligence, delusion and ignorance increase.

Thus different characteristics indicate the predominance of each guna.

Fruits of Gunas

"The fruit of good actions is said to be sātavik (goodness) and pure, the fruit of Rajas (passion) is pain, the fruit of dullness is ignorance."

[Verse 16 – Chapter XIV]

"From goodness arises knowledge and from passion greed, and from dullness, negligence, folly and ignorance arise.

[Verse 17 Chapter – XIV]

The above verses indicate the consequences of actions performed under the influence of the predominance of three gunas.

Sattavik actions lead to purity and knowledge. Action of Rajsic nature produce pain and greed. Dullness produces ignorance, error and negligence.

Obviously, it is desirable to cultivate sattavik nature and perform good actions.

Rise of the Soul

"When the embodied soul rises above the three gunas that spring from the body, it is freed from birth, death, old age, pain and attains life eternal."

[Verse 20 – Chapter XIV]

A body is evolved out of three modes of nature (prakriti) The soul assumes closeness with there modes producing attachment to external objects and states etc. This becomes the cause of birth, old age, pain and death. When the soul gradually makes progress on the spiritual path, it rises above these modes and thus gets freed from the bondage of birth and death and their evil consequences. All sufferings and pain of old age etc. are removed and it attains liberation.

Characteristics of a Liberated Soul

"He, who considers pain and pleasure alike, dwells in his own self, who views a clod, a stone, a piece of gold, as of equal worth, who remains the same amidst the pleasant and the unpleasant, is firm and regards blame and praise as one."

[Verse 24 – Chapter XIV]

"He, who is the same in honour and dishonour and is the same to friends and foes, who has abandoned all craving for activities, and is said to have resin above the three modes."

[Verse 25 – Chapter XIV]

"He, who worships Me with unfailing devotion of love, rises above the three modes, is fit for liberation."

[Verse 26 – Chapter XIV]

The above verses show the characteristics of a person (soul) who has risen above the three modes of nature. A man of there marks attains eternal wisdom which leads to liberation. The way to rise above the three modes of nature lies through love and unfailing devotion of God.

Soul – A Fraction of God

"A fragment (frction) of My own self, having become a living soul, eternal in the life of universe, draws to itself the senses of which mind is the sixth, that rest in nature."

[Verse 7 – Chapter XV]

The soul in the individual is a fraction of God. When embodied, it associates with the mind and the senses, which are born of nature (prakriti).

This verse has caused some controversy as there is another view which says that God is indivisible and therefore cannot be fragmented.

Perhaps, it may be concluded that God has close relationship with the individual soul which when embodied gets attracted towards mind and the senses and becomes deluded.

The Subtle Body Accompanies the Soul

"As the wind carries scent from its place, the individual soul (lord of the body) when leaves the body takes away the senses and the mind from the body which it leaves behind."

[Verse 8 – Chapter XV]

When the soul is in the body, it gets attracted to the mind and the senses. This association arising out of attachment continues even when the soul leaves the physical body and carries with it the mind and the senses as the wind takes away perfume from its base. Thus, the soul carries with it, these associates (mind and the senses) in its wanderings through cosmic existence, which the physical body is left behind and is burnt or burried underground.

The Perishable and the Imperishable

"There are two PURUSAS (persons) in this world – the perishable and the imperishable. All these existances are perishable while the unchanging is called imperishable."

[Verse 16 – Chapter XV]

The world is divided into two aspects, the perishable objects, such as the body etc. and the imperishable soul which exists in the body. It is because of the soul, which is the eternal living entity, that the body and its organs function. The soul is imperishable and when its leaves the body, the latter perishes. The imperishable soul never undergoes any modification.

Two Types of Beings

"There are two types of beings created in this world, the DIVINE and the Demoniac...

[Verse 6 Chapter XVI]

Broadly speaking all beings in this world can be classified in two types – Divine and Demoniac, in simple words, good and bad.

Verse 2-3 of the same chapter describe the qualities of persons of divine nature. There are as follows:-

Non-violence, truth, freedom from anger, renunciation tranquility, aversion to fault finding, compassion to living beings, freedom from greed, gentleness, modesty and steadiness, vigour, forgiveness, fortitude, purity, freedom from malice and excessive pride.

There are the distinctive qualities of those, who are seeking the divine perfection. We should, therefore cultivate divine qualities.

The Demoniac

"Ostentation, arrogance, excessive pride, anger as also harshness and ignorance, there are the endowment of persons of demoniac nature."

[Verse 4 – Chapter XVI]

Verses 2-3 describes the qualities of persons of divine nature. The above verse states the traits of persons of demoniac nature.

Verse 5 of the same chapter states the consequences of having these nature.

The divine qualities bad to liberation.

The demoniac traits lead to bondage and evil consequences. We should, therefore, shake off the demoniac traits and make all efforts to adopt divine qualities which lead to good results.

Three Kinds of Food

"The Foods which promote life, vitality, strength, health, joy and cheerfulness, which are sweet, soft, nourishing and agreeahle are dear to the good (SĀTVIK) people."

[Verse 8 – Chapter XVII]

"The foods that are bitter, sour, saltish, very hot, pungent, harsh and burning, producing pain, grief and disease are liked by the Rajsik type of people."

[Verse 9 – Chapter XVII]

"That which is spoiled, tasteless, half-ripe, putrid, stale, polluted and impure is the food dear to the dull (Tamsik)

[Verse 10 – Chapter XVIII]

The nature of a person, whether he is good (Sātvik), passionate (Rajsik), dull (Tamsik) can be judged from the type of food he likes and eats. The type of food one eats has great effect upon his mind and actions. The best type of food is Sātvik, which promote health, strength and joy. Such foods belong to the vegetarian category. Other food, as mentioned in the above verses fall in the Rajsik and Tamsik category. Thus, foods may be classified in these categories according to these are liked by people of different natures, i.e. Sātvik, Rajsik or Tamsik.

The Triple Gate of Hell

"LUST, ANGER and GREED are the gates to HELL and these ruin the SOUL. Therefore, one should avoid these."

[Verse 21 - Chapter XVI]

This is a very significant verse.

The above three tracts, lust (desire) anger and greed lead to the complete delusion of the soul. Lust which in broad sense means desire is the root cause of greed and anger.

Desire leads to attachment and greed. When desire remains unfulfilled, anger is produced. Similarly, when greed is not satisfied, dejection and anger are produced. All these three lead to delusion, ignorance and bondage and the soul gets enslaved and becomes helpless and then complete demoniac nature prevails. This is the cause of the ruin of the soul. We should, therefore, shun all these evil traits which lead to destruction and evil consequences. ❖✪❖

Three Kinds of Faith

"GOOD men (SĀTVIK) worship GOD, the passionate (RJSIK) worship the demigods, the dull (TAMSIK) worship the spirits and ghosts (forces of darkness)".

[Verse 4 – Chapter XVII]

All human beings are influenced by three modes (gunas). Sattava, Rajas and Tamas.

Those, who are good, have sātvik nature, cultivate divine qualities. Accordingly, they worship the All-pervading God with love and devotion.

Men of passionate (Rajsik) nature worship demigods (duties) to satisfy their selfish desires.

The ignorant (Tamsik) people worship spirits and ghosts. Their worship is of destructive nature.

The Sātvik worship is the best as it leads to libration. ❖✪❖

Three Kinds of Sacrifice (Yajna)

"Sacrifice (Yajna) which is performed according to scriptural law, by those who expect no reward and believe firmly that it is their duty to offer the sacrifice is good (SĀTVIK)"

[Verse II – Chapter XVII]

Sacrifice (Yajna) performed in good faith and according to laws of dharma (righteousness) is considered as a noble action. This is offered as a matter of one's duty and not for any selfish gain or reward. It is performed as an offering to the supreme Lord and results in general welfare. This is pure action in which a person dedicates his full devotion to the LORD and will even accept death gladly.

"But that which is offered in expectation of reward or for the sake of ostentation, is passionate (Rajsik) sacrifice.

[Verse 12 – Chapter XVII]

A sacrifice (Yajna) which is performed with a selfish motive to gain some reward or as display of outwards devotion etc. is of passionate (Rajsik) nature.

"That which is not in conformity with the spiritual law, in which no food is offered, no mantras are chanted, no donation is made and which is without faith, that sacrifice (Yajna) is of the nature of ignorance (Tamsik).

[Verse 13 – Chapter XVII]

In the performance of Yajna, certain rites (Agnihotra) is performed, hymns are chanted, donation is made and some food (Prasad) is offered to the gathering such yajna is performed with full faith and devotion. However, where these things are absent, such a Yajna is of passionate (Tamsik) nature. Such an exercise is born out of ignorance and is an unsocial and irreligious act.

It will be seen from above verses that sacrifice (Yajna) of Sātvik nature is the best, of Rajsik nature is inferior and of Tamsik nature is forbidden and undesirable.

Three Kinds of Penance (Tapa) (तप)

"WORSHIP of the gods, the Brahmanas, of teachers, of teachers and of the vise, purity, uprightness, celibacy and non-violence, are called the penance of the body."
"The spoken words which give no offence, which are truthful, pleasant and beneficial and the regular recitation of the Vedas – there are said to be the penance of SPEECH."
"Serenity of mind, gentleness, calmners, contemplation, self-control, purity of mind, are called the penance of MIND.

[Verses 14-16 – Chapter XVII]

The above three verses indicate the penance of three types, of body, speech and mind. These are worthy of practice for spiritual advancement. Verses 17-19 indicate the nature of different types of penance, performed under the influence of modes (gunas) Sātvik penance is that which is performed as a matter of duty and without expectation of reward.

Rajsik penance is performed for the sake of show or for gaining fame, honour and reverence.

Tamsik penance is performed with foolish obstinacy by self-torture or for harming others.

Penance of Sātvik nature is the best.

The Supreme Devotion

"Having become one with BRAHMA and being tranquil in spirit, he neither grieves nor desires and regarding all beings alike, he acquires supreme devotion to Me."

[Verse 54 - Chapter XVIII]

A devotee who has attained perfection reaches God and his mind becomes peaceful, free from any grief or desire. He remains calm and cheerful. Having realised his identity with God, he regards all beings alike as God is alike to all beings. Likewise, he develops a unique closeness with God and thus attains supreme devotion to Him.

Three Kinds of Gifts [Charity]

"CHARITY" made to one from whom no return is expected, with the feeling that it is one's duty to give, and which is given at a proper place and time and to a desecrving person, is considered as good (Sātvik).

[Verse 20 – Chapter XVII]

CHARITY (donation) gift etc. should be made, as a matter of duty and without any expectation of return, to a deserving person at a proper time and place. There is no selfish motive involved in sātvik (good) charity.

"CHARITY made in expectation of a return or reward or in a grudging manner is said to be passionate (Rajsik)"

[Verse 21 – Chapter XVII]

If charity is made with some selfish motive or under some compulsion or when it hurts the griever, this is Rajsik Charity.

"And when charity is made at a wrong place and time to an undeserving person, without any respect, or with contempt, it is considered tamsik (made out of ignorance)"

[Verse 22 – Chapter XVII]

It will be seen from above verses that the sātvik charity, donation or gift is of highest kind. We should make charity of this kind.

Do your own Duty

"Better is one's own duty through imperfectly done than the duty of another though done perfectly. One does not incur sin when one performs the duty ordained by one's own nature."

[Verse 47 - Chapter XVIII]

One should perform one's duty in accordance with one's own nature, even if it is imperfect or faulty. Man's own duty is born out of his innate nature which is formed according to the presence of three modes (gunas). Duty performed according to one's own nature is better than the duty of others. It is not beneficial employing our minds in actions which are not based on our intrinsic nature. The above verse tells us that the duty performed according to one's own innate nature does not incur sin. This is the right way to avoid any sin.

Three Kinds of Knowledge

Verse 20 to 22 of Chapter XVIII of the *Gita* mention three types of knowledge, summarised as follows:-

I. True knowledge that leads to god-realisation and promotes righteousness is Sātvik (good). As a result of this knowledge, one GOD is seen in all existence.

II. The knowledge that leads to division and separateness in different creatures is Rajsik.

III. The knowledge that leads to ignorance and unreality is of the nature of dullness (Tamsik).

[Verses 20-22 of Chapter XVIII]

Sātvik knowledge that causes enlightenment and leads to God is the best and most desirable. The other two are far inferior. One must avoid knowledge that leads to ignorance and falsehood.

Three Kinds of Action

Three modes (gunas) affect the action, in the following ways:-

I. An obligatory action/duty performance without attachment, love or hate and without concern for its fruit is of the nature of goodness (Sātvik).

II. Action performed under strain and impelled by selfishness and for the gratification of desires is Rajsik (passionate nature).

III. Action performed out of ignorance and without any regard for consequences and one's human capacity is Tamsik (of dull nature).

[Verses 23-25 – Chapter XVIII]

It will be seen from the above descriptions that the Sātvik action arre the best.

Three Kinds of Understanding

Verses 30-32 indicate distinction between three kinds of understanding as follows:-

I. The understanding which discriminates between right and wrong, desirable and undesirable, which frees the Soul, that understanding is of the nature of goodness (Sātvik).

II. That which creates a wrong and mistaken impression and is misleading is Rajsik.

II. That which holds wrong as right and views all things in a perverted way, is Tamsik.

[Verse 30-32 – Chapter XVIII]

Sātvik understanding has the right and liberating approach. Rajsik understanding is misleading and has wrong perspective, while the Tamsik understanding is perverted and enveloped in darkness. We should cultivate Sātvik approach and follow the right way.

Give up Attachment and Desire

"But even these actions as also other duties should be performed giving up attachment and desire for fruits..."

[Verse 6 – Chapter XVIII]

It may be concluded from the above verse that certain actions and obligatory duties have to be performed. Acts in connections with one's profession, bodily acts, such as, eating, drinking, sleeping, walking, sitting etc. and other essential actions of daily life, have to be performed. Actions also have to be performed for general welfare of the society, country etc. What is emphasised here is that all such necessary actions and obligatory duties should be performed without attachment and desire for fruits of actions.

Three Kinds of Steadiness

I. Steadiness which is unwavering, controls the mind life breath and senses is Sātvik. This is possible through concentration.

II. That by which, one performs actions, desiring fruits pleasure and wealth is Rajsik.

III. Steadiness which induces sleep, grief, depression and arrogance is Tamsik.

[Verses 33-35 – Chapter XVIII]

Sātvik steadiness makes us aware of what our common understanding is unable to know.

Rajsik steadiness makes us run after material gains and comforts.

Tamsik steadiness promotes laziness, grief and similar other evil consequences.

A person of Sātvik steadiness remains detached which Rajsik and Tamsik steadiness promote attachment and thus bind the soul. ❖✪❖

Work is Workship

"He from whom all beings arise and by whom all this is pervaded – by worshipping HIM through the performance of his own duty does man attain perfection."

[Verse 46 - Chapter XVIII]

True worship of God lies in the performance of ones duty and this is the way to attain perfection. Every human being has some duties to perform. These duties may vary according to his birth, inborn nature, quality and capacity and the profession he practises. If he carries out his duties most devotedly and to the best of his ability and capacity, he is worshiping God truly by the performance of his duty. No formal religions rites are needed for this. That is why, it is said "Work is worship' and the work performed in this manner as one's essential duty becomes the means to attain perfection. ❖✪❖

Three Kinds of Happiness

Happiness is the universal aim of human life. The modes (gunas) which dominate our nature, lead to different kinds of happiness as mentioned below:-

I. That happiness in which one feels delight by long practice and where sorrow ends, which is like poison first but becomes nectar at the end, which springs from the charity of understanding, is Sātvik.

II. That which results from the gratification of sensual desires, which is like nectar at first but like poison at the end is Rajsik.

III. That which deludes the soul and arises out of ignorance, laziness and negligence is Tamsik.

[Verse 36-39 - Chapter XVIII]

True happiness comes from constant long practice of spiritual discipline which may involve restraint and pain in the begnning but leads to inner joy and freedom. One can pass from the happiness of true knowledge and moral values to eternal bliss. Rajsik happiness which comes from the enjoyment of worldly pleasures is of temporary nature and ends in sorrow. Tamsik happiness is ignorant about its evil consequences.

The forgoing examples show how three modes (gunas) of nature can influence human character and activities. These gunas, due to their respective influence keep the soul in bondage, as human beings continue to experience pleasure and pain on the basis of these gunas. Among these, the Sātvik gunas are the most desirable, the Rajsik, the most prevalent and the Tamsik, the most despicable and harmful. However, more acquisition of Sātvik gunas is not the ultimate stage of human development. This stage can act as a stepping stone to the attainment of the final goal of life, which lies in the eternal bliss. By constant practice of spiritual discipline over a long time, one can transcend the sātvik stage and rise to the ultimate stage of God-realisation.

Om (Aum) Tat Sat

"AUM TAT SAT" is considered to be threefold symbol of BRAHMAN. By this were ordained, the Brahmins, the VEDAS and the sacrifices (YAJNA).

[Verse 23 – Chapter XVII]

Om, Tat and Sat are the three names of God. At the beginning of the creation, God created the Vedas, the Brahmins and the sacrifices. The methods of sacrifices were explained in the Vedas and brahmins performed these sacrifices (Yajnas).

OM (AUM) expresses the absolute supremacy and universality of God.

TAT, the reality and SAT denotes the state of existence and goodness, SAT also indicates steadfastness in Yajna, Tapa and Dan. Om indicates eternal Brahman, Tat indicates Sātvik action and Sat means pure action.

OM is always uttered by the worshippers of Brahman, whenever they undertake any good action. Such is the importance of these glorious words.

Renunciation and Relinquishment

"The wise understand by 'renunciation', the giving up of actions prompted by desire, the learned declare that the abandonment of the fruits of actions is called relinquishment."

[Verse 2 – Chapter XVIII]

The above verse clearly indicates the destinction between renunciation (Sanyasa) and relinquishment (Tyaga). Renunciation involves giving up of actions which arise out of selfish desires. Relinquishment means having no desire for fruits of action. It means performing actions without desire for fruits.

Some wire men declare that all actions should be given up as an evil, while some others think that evil actions should be given up. Some philosophers declare that other actions may be given up but sacrifice (Yajna), gift (Dan) and penance (Tapa) should not be given up. It is felt that obligatory actions, such as maintenance of body etc. can not be given up.

The Relinquisher

"The man who has no aversion to disagreeable action and no attachment to agreeable one, is a man of true renunciation, is wise and he has all his doubts resolved and established in the self.

[Verse 10 – Chapter XVIII]

"It is indeed impossible for any embodied being to abandon actions entirely. But he who gives up fruits of actions is said to be the relinquishers.

[Verse 11 – Chapter XVIII]

Ordinarily, a man will like to perform actions which are pleasant and agreeable and will have dislike for those actions which are disagreeable. A true relinquisher has neither aversion nor attachment to corresponding actions. His relinquishment attains perfection as he is unaffected by these actions, whether agreeable or disagreeable.

An embodied being can not abandon actions because the body has evolved from nature (Prakriti) which is always active. The real relinquishment arises from the inner-self. External relinquishment is temporary and unreal. ❖✪❖

Spiritual Perfection

"He whose understnding is unattached alround, who has subdued his self and from whom desire has fled – he attains the supreme state through renunciation."

[Verse 49 – Chapter XVIII]

The above verse mentions the basic conditions which lead to the attainment of supreme state. These are as follows:-

I. Absence of attachment to things, actions persons, incidents, circumstances etc.

II. Absence of desire, a person should he satisfied with what he gets.

III. Control over body, mind and soul.

The fulfillment of these conditions produces inner renunciation which leads to the supreme state of spiritual perfection. ❖✪❖

Role of Three Modes (Gunas)

"There is no being on earth or again in heaven what is free from the three modes born of nature (Prakriti)"

[Verse 40 – Chapter XVIII]

"Three modes of nature (Prakriti) evolve out of nature (prakriti) which is ever active. There is, therefore, no creature in this universe that is free from the influence of these modes.
"OF Brahmins, Kshatryas and Vaishyas as also of Shudras, their activities (duties) are distinguished in accordance with the qualities (gunas) born of their nature."

[Verse 41 – Chapter XVIII]

The four-fold order of society is of universal application as it is bared on the types of human nature. It is not based on birth or heredity, as is wrongly interpreted by some vested interests. It is the dominating modes (gunas) of a person which determine to which category that person belongs. There are four broad types of nature which correspond to the four kinds of beings. This classification also changes increase the quality of modes (gunas) in an individual changes.

How to Attain Perfection

"Endowed with a pure understanding, firmly restraining the senses, turning away from sound and other objects of sense and casting aside attraction and aversion."

[Verse 51 – Chapter XVIII]

"Dwelling in solitude, eating but little, controlling speech body and mind, ever engaged in meditation and concentration and resorting to dispassion."

[Verse 52 – Chapter XIII]

"Having abandoned egoism, violence, arrogance, desire anger, covetousness and tranquil in mind, he becomes worthy of attaining Brahma."

[Verse 53 – Chapter XVIII]

The above three verses describe the virtues with which a devotee can attain Brahma (the Supreme POEing) All these virtues lead to the purification of the inner-self and prepare a striver to enable him to become perfectly fit to attain Brahma.

Four-Fold Classification Based on Modes (Gunas)

Verses 42-44 of Chapter XVIII of the *Gita* indicate the qualities (gunas) expected of there four classes, as follows:-

1. Brahmins : They are supposed to have the following gunas – serenity, self-control, austerity, purity, forgiveness, uprightness, knowledge (wisdom), faith in God and religion. Experiences of performance of sacrifice (Yajnk).
2. Kshatriyas : Heroism, vigour, steadiness, resource fulness not fleeing from battle, generosity, leadership are the natural qualities of a kshatriya.
3. Vaishyas : Agriculture, tendering cattle, trade are the duties of a vaishya.
4. Shudras : Activities consisting of service to the society are the characteristics of a shudra, born of his nature.

It is emphasised that there qualities are inborn and an intrinsic part of human nature of a particular person. These are though well-defined, yet can not be regarded as exclusive and are not determined always by birth or heredity. There are also changeable. A son of shudra, by virtue of his progress and development can rise to become a vaishya or kshatriya etc. and vice-verse.

The Way to Salvation

"Performing continually all actions whatsoever, taking refuge in Me. By My grace, My devotee reaches the eternal, undying state."

[Verse 56 – Chapter XVIII]

This verse tells us in a simple clear manner how to attain salvation. Salvation is the highest goal of human life. It is the state free from births and deaths, pleasure and pain, free from bondage, a state of eternal bliss. It is also the goal of Karmayaoga, where one has to perform his duty which taking refuge in God. He has to take refuge in God by practising from faith in Him. In this manner, he will attract God's grace which will lead him to salvation.

The Way to Reach God

"Mentally dedicating all actions to ME, regarding Me as the SUPREME goal and resorting to steadfastness in understanding, do than fix thy mind constantly on Me."

[Verse 57 – Chapter XVIII]

The above verse depicts a four-point action plan to reach God, as follows:-

1. Mentally surrender all actions to God. God has given you body, mind, senses, intellect etc and you are His agent to make proper use of these instruments, without any egoism.
2. Regard God as the supreme goal of your life.
3. Remain firm and steadfast in right understanding.
4. In this way, fix your mind constantly on Me.

God becomes the supreme goal, the focus of all attention and the object of worship and constant rememberances. This is well-planned approach to reach God.

The Final Words

"Abandoning dependence on all duties, take refuge in ME alone, I shall release you from evils."

[Verse 66 – Chapter XVIII]

The Lord concludes his instructions in this verse. Arjuna was perturbed by the various duties imposed by him on himself on ethical and social grounds and the consequences of the impending war and thus was confused about his role. Lord Krishna tells him clearly not to worry about these and provides him with a solution which lies in the whole-hearted surrender to Him alone. Total unconditional surrender to the Supreme,with absolute faith and complete devotion raises us to our utmost level of perfection and thus attracts the grace of GOD who releases us from all evils, pain and misery. This is the highest attainment of a devotee, who serves Him alone, in this manner.

Conclusion

"This famous Gitasastra (Bhagavad GITA) is an epitome of the essentials of the whole Vedic teaching. A knowledge of its teaching leads to the realisation of all human aspirations."

[Adi Sankaracharya]

The *Gita* being the source of true knowledge and wisdom, acts as the supreme teacher which provides great guidance in all aspects of human life. In the words of Swami Sivananda, it is an inexhaustible spiritual treasure and an ocean of knowledge. The knowledge contained in the *Gita* is not confined within the four walls of a particular sect or traditional religion. It is meant for people of all temperaments and for all times, without any distinction of caste, creed, community, country and gender etc. It has universal approach and application.

The various divine virtues as mentioned in the *Gita* can transform a genuine devotee, from a weahling to a worthy, strong, peaceful purposeful and successful person. The teachings contained I these selected verses can lead to true wisdom and right understanding of real goal of human life. Having understood and analysed the import of their right meaning, one can reach the highest stage which transcends all pain and misery. The *Gita* explains the practical paths of yoga of action, knowledge and devition along with the methods of concentration and meditation. These paths which can lead to the highest stage of perfection are not separate water-tight compartments. The practical and useful approach lies through a synthesis of all these yogic disciplines. Selfless action, right knowledge and complete devotion to the Supreme – all these have to be practised in harmony, in all walks of human life.

For those, who do not find sufficient time to reach the whole of the *Gita*, this small volume of only selected verses will come handy and easy to read and understand. It will be both useful and desirable, that some of these verses should be read everyday in the morning and in the evening. Of course, these can be read at any other suitable time of the day, as may be found convenient and practicable. However, it may be patinent to point out here, that these verses from the *Gita* are not meant just for reading, reciting and reverence only. The message which these verses convey and the teaching which they contain are meant to be actually practised in everyday life. More parrot like reading, without their practical application, will be of no avail.

In conclusion, it may be said that all essential aspects of human life and the means to attain the highest goal of life are briefly explained in these selected verses, for quick absorption and actual practice. It may be kept in view, what Swamy Parthasarthy, a modern philosopher and a great exponent of the *Gita*, had said – 'The *Gita* is a plan for Action, not for retirement.'

The *Gita* shows the way to rise to the highest goal from the abyss of ignorance. It is for us to make a choice and to tread the right path.